THE CIVIL RIGHTS MOVEMENT

By Stuart Kallen

Visit us at
www.abdopub.com

Published by ABDO Publishing Company, 4940 Viking Drive, Edina, MN 55435.
Copyright © 2001 by Abdo Consulting Group, Inc. International copyrights reserved in all countries. No part of this book may be reproduced in any form without written permission from the publisher.

Printed in the United States.

Edited by: Paul Joseph
Graphic Design: City Desktop Productions

Cover Photos: Corbis
Interior Photos: Corbis

Library of Congress Cataloging-in-Publication Data

Kallen, Stuart A., 1955 -
      The Civil Rights Movement / Stuart Kallen.
          p. cm. -- (Black History)
      Includes index.
      ISBN 1-57765-466-8
      1. Afro-Americans--Civil rights--History--20th century--Juvenile
literature. 2. Civil rights movements--United States--History--20th
century--Juvenile literature. [1. Afro-Americans--Civil rights. 2.
Civil rights movements.] I. Title.

E185.61 .K338 2001
323.1'196073--dc21   00-056890

CONTENTS

Frightened African-American girls flee police during a race riot.

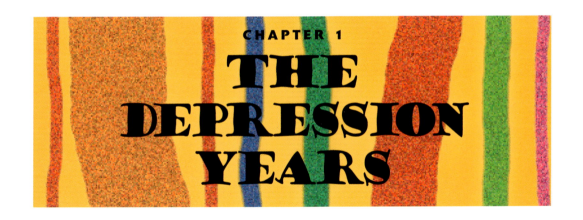

CHAPTER 1

THE DEPRESSION YEARS

Last Hired, First Fired

In October 1929, the stock market crashed. Millions of Americans were thrust into poverty. But months before this, many black people knew that the economy was in trouble. Every day, black newspapers wrote about huge layoffs of black workers. These workers were often "the last to be hired and the first to be fired." They did not need a newspaper to know that something was wrong.

Great Depression homeless stand in line, 1930.

The booming economy of the 1920s helped more black people find decent jobs. But the stock market crash began the worst depression in American history. By 1931, one out of every three blacks was unemployed. In cities like Atlanta, Georgia, 80 percent of the black people needed public relief, or welfare. But relief was nowhere in sight. Agencies that helped the poor were not able to assist everyone. Soup kitchens and homeless shelters turned away black people. Government relief programs gave larger allowances to whites than blacks. For black people, the fight against racism had to be put on hold. Suddenly, there was a new enemy to fight—starvation.

The New Deal

Herbert Hoover, a Republican, was president when the Depression began. Until that time, most black people had voted for the Republican Party. Abraham Lincoln, the first Republican president,

President Franklin Roosevelt

was considered a hero for his role in ending slavery.

In 1932, Hoover ran against Franklin Delano Roosevelt, a Democrat. To many, Hoover seemed unconcerned about the plight of blacks. But Roosevelt tried hard to reach black voters. Most blacks decided to vote for "bread and butter instead of the memory of Abraham Lincoln." Roosevelt was elected, and the New Deal began.

A Mardi Gras celebration in relief decorates the facade of the Louisiana state capitol building in Baton Rouge. The capitol's reliefs were created as a Works Progress Administration (WPA) project in the 1930s.

Roosevelt set up agencies to help relieve the effects of the Depression. He made sure that black people were included. These agencies included the Works Progress Administration (WPA) and the Civilian Conservation Corps (CCC). They gave training and jobs to hundreds of thousands of black people. Roosevelt also set up agencies to employ writers, actors, musicians, and photographers. The Federal Writers' Project employed many well-known black writers. The Federal Theatre Project sponsored many interracial and all-black plays in cities all over the country.

Hundreds of thousands of black children enrolled in classes through the National Youth Administration (NYA). Many thousands

African-American Civilian Conservation Corps (CCC) enrollees fill in a gully on eroded farm land.

A National Youth Administration defense worker student at Bethune-Cookman College.

of black adults learned new skills through other programs. These workers built black schools and hospitals. They also built community centers and playgrounds. President Roosevelt was very popular among black voters. Many blacks called him the "Great White Father."

Roosevelt also welcomed college-educated blacks into the highest ranks of the government.

Welding class for National Youth Administration (NYA) students attending Bethune-Cookman College.

By 1938, his "Black Cabinet" included over 20 experts in many different areas. These experts advised Roosevelt on what black people wanted and expected from the government. They demanded equal rights for everyone. These experts also helped black people to realize that they were a vital part of American society.

The movement toward equality made great progress while Roosevelt was president. But blacks were still treated unfairly, even within the federal government. Racism continued in many programs that were designed to help the poor. Violence against black people persisted throughout the 1930s. For the poorest Americans, many of whom were black, the Depression made life harder than ever.

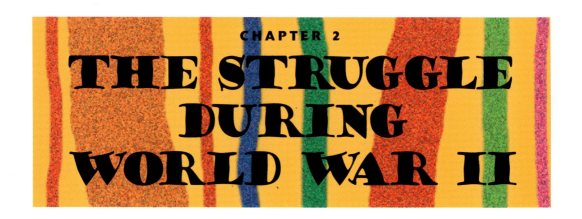

CHAPTER 2

THE STRUGGLE DURING WORLD WAR II

Demands for Equal Opportunity

In 1939, World War II began in Europe. The United States did not join the fight until 1941. Before then, however, American industries worked hard to supply the Allies with materials for war.

Many factories that made war materials refused to hire black workers. To protest this, the National Association for the Advancement of Colored People (NAACP) organized a march on Washington, D.C. The march was to take place on July 1, 1941. President Roosevelt promised to take action if the march was canceled. Black leaders agreed. On June 25, Roosevelt signed Executive Order 8802. This order banned discrimination in industries that had government contracts. Roosevelt also set up a special committee to make sure the order was obeyed.

Patriotism and Prejudice

In December 1941, the United States entered World War II. President Roosevelt said that the war was being fought for the Four Freedoms: freedom of speech, freedom of religion, freedom from want, and freedom from fear. Many black Americans rushed to join this fight. But often they had to face bias at home before they could fight the enemy across the ocean.

Before World War II, the armed forces were strictly segregated. Most blacks in the Navy worked only in the food services. In the Army, blacks were kept in all-black units. Blacks could not enter the Air Force or the Marines. The American Red Cross even segregated the blood in its blood banks. Although both blacks and whites were required to serve in the armed forces, they did not receive equal treatment.

African-Americans man an artillery site during World War II.

In 1940, the United States began increasing the size of its military. In September of that year, three black leaders traveled to Washington. They urged Roosevelt to end segregation in the armed forces. They wanted black recruits to receive the same training as whites. They argued that blacks should be able to become officers. They also demanded that black doctors and nurses be integrated into the services.

The government took action. In 1941, the Army accepted blacks for unsegregated training. In 1942, the Navy and Marines allowed blacks to join as equals. The Air Force opened a special post for the training of black pilots. Black women were also accepted. The Army Air Corps began training black pilots at Tuskegee Institute. These Tuskegee airmen became famous for their bravery and superb flying skills. They earned over 800 medals for their contributions. Overall, more than one million blacks served in World War II.

"Jim Crow" at Home

Around 1830, a white singer named Thomas Rice grew famous for painting his face black and performing a song called "Jump, Jim Crow." As a result of this song, the name "Jim Crow" was often associated with segregation.

Jim Crow Segregation

Laws that prevented black people from using white facilities were called Jim Crow laws.

During World War II, many states still had Jim Crow laws. Langston Hughes wrote, "Blacks who wanted to serve their country did so at the risk of their dignities and sometimes at the risk of their lives, long before they met the official enemy. The enemy that hurt them the worst was Jim Crow. Jim Crow ignored their citizenship and scorned them as human beings."

Symbolic Death of Jim Crow—African-American men carry a coffin and a "Here Lies Jim Crow" sign down the middle of a street as a demonstration against "Jim Crow" segregation laws.

During the war, thousands of black people moved north to work in defense plants. More than 50,000 blacks moved to Detroit in two years. Housing became a problem everywhere. Many whites did not want black people to move into their neighborhoods. Race riots broke out in many cities, including Detroit, New York, and Mobile, Alabama.

CHAPTER 3

GIFTED BLACKS IN THE 30s AND 40s

Joe Louis (1914–1981)

Boxer

Joe Louis Barrow was born in a one-room shack in Chamber County, Alabama. By the age of four, he was already working in the cotton fields beside his mother and father. During his childhood, Joe's father died and his mother remarried. Her new husband went to Detroit to find work, and later sent for his family. Joe's family was still poor, but in Detroit they had indoor plumbing and electric lights.

Joe began to box when he was a teenager. He was knocked down seven times during his first bout. But within two years he had won

Joe Louis

48 out of 54 fights. He dropped the Barrow from his name and began to use the name Joe Louis.

In 1934, Louis decided to become a professional boxer. But most white fighters would not fight against a black man. During interracial fights, riots often broke out if the black man won. But by 1935, Louis was becoming well known as a fighter. That year, he boxed against Primo Carnera, the six-foot-six "Man Mountain." The fight was held at Yankee Stadium in New York. Over 1,500 policemen surrounded the stadium to prevent riots. When Louis knocked out Carnera in the eighth round, thousands of blacks jammed the streets of Harlem to celebrate.

The next year, Louis was scheduled to fight a German boxer, Max Schmeling, who was a favorite of Adolf Hitler. Hitler thought Schmeling would help show that Germans were better than blacks. Louis set out to prove Hitler wrong, but he came up short. When Schmeling knocked out Louis in the twelfth round, hundreds of black people wept in the streets.

In 1937, Louis beat James Braddock to become the heavyweight champion. In 1938, he fought Schmeling again and floored him in the first round. Once again, millions of people celebrated Louis' victory.

After four years in the army and a few more fights, Louis retired from boxing in 1951. He was the heavyweight champion for almost

Joe Louis & Max Schmeling— Second fight.

12 years, longer than any other fighter. Joe Louis was an inspiration to black people all over the country. His fame was a shining light during the darkness of the Depression.

Richard Wright (1908–1960)

Author

Richard Wright was born in Mississippi. When he was four, he accidentally set his house on fire and was beaten so badly that he almost died. Hunger and poverty were all that Richard knew as a boy. His father abandoned his family when Richard was five. After that, he lived with relatives in Tennessee and Arkansas. He also spent time in an orphanage.

After Wright's mother suffered a stroke, the family went to live with his grandparents in Jackson, Mississippi. In Jackson, Wright attended school and learned to read. His love of reading inspired him to be an author, but his grandparents discouraged him. They said that a black man could never make a living as an author.

Wright spent his years in Jackson working at menial jobs. In desperation, he stole a gun and some food. He sold the gun and bought a train ticket to Memphis. In Memphis, Wright worked in an optical shop.

Richard Wright

He borrowed a library card from a friendly white man and began reading whenever he could.

In 1927, Wright moved to Chicago. When the Depression began, he found himself unemployed. In 1937, Wright moved to New York City, where he published a book of stories called *Uncle Tom's Children*. In 1940, Wright published *Native Son*. *Native Son* told of how prejudice in the North affected a young black man. Within three weeks, the book sold over 250,000 copies. Wright became famous. He soon published *Twelve Million Black Voices* and *Black Boy*, a book about his terrible childhood.

Wright moved to Paris. He continued to write novels that described the real lives of poor blacks in America. Millions of people have benefited from the knowledge they gained from Richard Wright's books.

Charles Richard Drew (1904–1950)

Doctor, Scientist

During World War II, a surgeon named Charles Richard Drew invented a way to separate whole blood from blood plasma. This discovery meant that blood could be stored for much longer periods of time. Dr. Drew's process made blood available to people who were wounded during the Nazi bombing of England in 1940. Because of his work, thousands of lives were saved.

Drew became the director of the Red Cross program that collected blood for the U.S. Armed Forces. The military, however, would not accept black people's blood. When Drew protested, the military agreed to change their policy. But they insisted that blood from nonwhite donors be kept separate from white donors' blood. This racist policy caused Drew to resign from the program in 1942. He became a surgeon and professor of medicine in Washington, D.C. He died in a car accident in 1950.

Jackie Robinson (1919–1972)

Baseball Player

At UCLA, Jackie Robinson, played basketball, baseball, and football. He was also a track star. Robinson became the first athlete ever to earn letters in four different sports. In 1942, he enlisted in the Army. He enrolled in officer training school and became a second lieutenant.

After the war, Robinson joined a baseball team in the Negro Leagues. In August 1945, Branch Rickey signed Robinson to play for the Brooklyn Dodgers. In 1947, Robinson became the first black player in the major leagues. He faced threats and jeers wherever he went. Many of his teammates asked that he be removed from the team. The Philadelphia Phillies and the St. Louis Cardinals refused to play against Robinson and the Dodgers. But Rickey and Ford Frick, the National League President, supported Robinson. In 1947, the Dodgers won the National League pennant. Robinson was named Rookie of the Year. He was named MVP in 1949 and retired in 1957. After retirement, he became a successful businessman. He was also active in politics and the movement for civil rights. Jackie Robinson joined the Baseball Hall of Fame in 1962.

Jackie Robinson poses in his batting stance. Robinson became a spokesman for black Americans and was the first African American inducted into the National Baseball Hall of Fame.

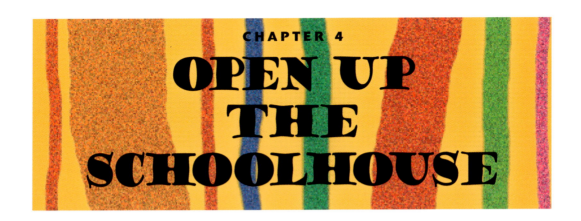

CHAPTER 4

OPEN UP THE SCHOOLHOUSE

Thousands of black people died for the cause of freedom during World War II. But when the war ended, America's blacks continued to face Jim Crow laws, poor schools, unfair housing, and daily prejudice. In several southern states, most black people were still denied the right to vote. In the early 1950s, black taxpayers were still not allowed to attend state-supported universities.

President Harry Truman

19

Black people found a supporter in President Harry S. Truman. When Truman ran for vice-president in 1944, he supported a federal antilynching bill, fair hiring practices, and equal rights for black voters. When Truman became president in 1945, he established the Civil Rights Commission. In his 1948 State of the Union address, Truman became the first president to make "full human rights" for blacks a national goal. He also asked Congress to make workplaces and public transportation fair for all people.

Congress did not pass the laws that Truman requested. Some northern states, however, enacted bills of their own. By 1948, several states had outlawed discrimination in housing, schools, public transportation, restaurants, and theaters. These laws were not always enforced, but they marked another step on the road to equality.

The Battle over Schools

In 1896, the Supreme Court heard the case *Plessy v. Ferguson*. In it, the Court ruled that it was legal for public facilities to be "separate but equal." This meant that blacks could be kept apart from whites, as long as equal facilities were provided for both. In fact, though, black schools, train cars, and restrooms were almost always much worse than those for whites. Black schools in the South were usually rundown shacks with few books and supplies.

On May 17, 1954, the Supreme Court ruled that American schools could no longer be "separate but equal." Two weeks later, the Court ordered 17 states with segregated schools to integrate them immediately.

This decision began a huge battle in the South. The governors of South Carolina, Georgia, and Mississippi were opposed to the idea of school integration. They threatened to abolish public schools, rather than let blacks and whites attend the same classes. One hundred members of Congress signed a petition against the ruling. In Virginia, white politicians and ministers threatened "massive resistance" to school integration.

A young child walks with his angry mother as she removes him from his school in Alabama which had just become desegregated.

The Fight in Arkansas

A high school in Little Rock, Arkansas, became the focus of the fight over school integration. In 1955, a black newspaper publisher named Daisy Bates led the NAACP's campaign to allow black students to attend all-white Central High. Many people were strongly opposed to Bates's plan. People threw rocks and fired guns at the windows of her home. The school board offices were bombed. Forty-four teachers who favored Bates's plan were fired. Her newspaper was forced to close.

Two years later, nine black students were admitted to Central High. But before they could attend classes, they needed help from the Supreme Court, the President, the Army, and the Arkansas State Militia.

The Governor Blocks the Doors

On September 4, 1957, the governor of Arkansas, Orval Faubus, posted the Arkansas National Guard in front of Central High. They blocked the school's entrance with their rifles and prevented the black students from entering. Racists in the crowd yelled obscenities and threatened the lives of blacks.

A court battle went on for many weeks. Governor Faubus was ordered to remove the National Guard from the school. President

President Dwight D. Eisenhower

Dwight Eisenhower met with Faubus. He asked the governor to allow the black students to enter, but Faubus still refused.

On September 23, the Little Rock Nine, as they were known, returned to the school. Four black reporters went with them. Police cars carrying the students and reporters arrived seconds before the morning bell. The crowd attacked the black reporters, thinking that they were the students' parents. Three ran away, but Alex Wilson, editor of the *Chicago Defender,* was hit in the head with a brick. Meanwhile, the nine students sneaked in the side door of the school. When the mob realized this, they turned their anger on white reporters. Journalists and photographers from *Life* magazine were beaten and their cameras were destroyed. People in the crowd screamed, cursed, and wept as the black students looked out the school windows.

Calling Out the Army

That evening, Eisenhower ordered 1,000 men from the 101st Airborne Division to go to Little Rock. On September 24, a convoy of jeeps with machine guns transported the children to school. Helicopters circled overhead as students climbed the steps into the school. Once inside, each student was given a bodyguard. After school, each student was escorted home.

For the next several years, Orval Faubus tried to thwart the Supreme Court order by shutting down the schools completely. Most white students attended private schools, leaving blacks with nowhere to go. By 1962, Arkansas finally integrated its schools.

Governor
Orval Faubus

Little Rock Nine

CHAPTER 5

MOVING TO THE FRONT

If black people did not like the segregated seating at a movie theater or restaurant, they could refuse to go to such places. But many blacks had to ride city buses to and from work. The racist rules of southern bus companies were a fact of life for many blacks until 1955.

In the South, black people paid their fares at the front of the bus. Then they moved to a separate section at the back of the bus. They had to leave through the back doors. If the black section was full, black people had to stand, even if there were empty seats in the white section. If the white section was full, black people had to give their seats to white people. This situation became one of the first battlegrounds in the fight for desegregation.

Rosa Parks Keeps Her Seat

On December 1, 1955, Rosa Parks, a 42-year-old black woman, boarded a bus in Montgomery, Alabama. Parks was the secretary of the local NAACP. She sat in the middle section, where blacks could sit until the white seats filled up. When several white men got on the bus, the bus driver told Parks to move so that the white men could have her seat. Parks refused. She was arrested for violating Jim Crow laws.

News of Parks's arrest soon reached Edgar Daniel Nixon. Nixon was a former head of the local NAACP. He had been trying for years to end Montgomery's bus discrimination. Nixon wanted to organize a boycott of the bus company. This meant that blacks would refuse to ride the buses until they were guaranteed equal treatment. Nixon thought that if the bus company stopped receiving money from black riders, they would have to change their policy.

When Parks was arrested, Nixon saw his chance. He called 19 black ministers in Montgomery and organized a bus boycott. Black college students handed out over 35,000 flyers. The flyers explained why Rosa Parks had been arrested. They also asked every black person to refuse to ride city buses on December 5, the day of Parks' trial.

Rosa Parks riding the bus.

The flyers circulated secretly through Montgomery's schools, bars, churches, and stores. Secrecy was important, because many people were afraid of losing their jobs or being lynched.

Dr. King Steps In

On Monday, the buses were empty. Black people owned 18 taxi companies in Montgomery. These companies agreed to transport blacks for 10 cents, the same fare as the bus. Monday night, thousands of people gathered in their churches to rally against segregation. A new reverend in town, Dr. Martin Luther King, Jr., gave a fiery speech to the boycotters. Thousands of people listened in the churches and through loudspeakers in the streets. It was decided that the boycott would last until segregation ended.

After four days city officials declared that they would not accept the blacks' demands. In response, Dr. King organized a carpool network. Blacks who owned cars agreed to drive others to work. Many white employers offered their cars for support. Local leaders set up the Montgomery Improvement Association (MIA) to organize the boycott and collect funds. King was named president of this group. Before long, the MIA carpools were picking up workers at 42 locations. For the next 13 months, empty buses drove through the streets of Montgomery.

On January 30, Dr. King's house was firebombed. His wife, Coretta, hid in a back room with their seven-month-old baby. No one was injured. On February 1, Edgar Nixon's house was firebombed. He too escaped injury. On February 12, King and 24 other ministers were arrested under an Alabama law that prohibited boycotts. King was convicted and fined $500. When he was released to appeal the case, King began touring the country to raise money for the boycott. Everywhere he went, people marveled at his beautiful and thoughtful speeches.

Victory!

The case against Rosa Parks finally went to the United States Supreme Court. The Court struck down the Jim Crow laws. On December 21, 1956, blacks began riding the Montgomery buses again. This time they sat wherever they wanted. By this time, though, other battles were being waged in Montgomery. White terrorists fired shots at buses and firebombed black churches and black people's homes. Dr. King continued to preach a message of nonviolence. He began organizing boycotts in cities all over the South.

Martin Luther King, Jr. on a Montgomery Bus—December 21, 1956.

CHAPTER 6

RIDING TO FREEDOM

By 1960, there was a new generation of black college students. These students were old enough to remember the Little Rock school protests and the Montgomery bus boycott. Their parents may have settled for the Jim Crow way of life, but these young people would not. After the bus boycott, Dr. King and others formed new organizations. The Southern Christian Leadership Conference (SCLC) and the Congress for Racial Equality (CORE) were two of the main groups. They taught black students and others how to hold nonviolent protests. Across the South, these groups held sit-ins, boycotts, pickets, and protests.

Four college students held the first sit-in at a lunch counter on February 1, 1960. Over the next year, around 70,000 people participated in sit-ins around the South. When a restaurant refused to serve black people, protesters filled the seats and stayed for hours, until no customers had room to sit down. When police arrested everyone at the counter, another group of protesters sat down. Wave after wave of protesters blocked the lunch counter until the jails were full.

Three students from North Carolina A&T College (an all black school) refuse to leave a lunch counter reserved for whites at Woolworth's in Greensboro, North Carolina.

This plan worked. Before long, blacks were being served at restaurants. Black students began to focus on other segregated places. They held read-ins at white libraries, kneel-ins at white churches, and even sleep-ins at white hotels. The police responded by arresting hundreds of blacks. Judges gave protesters large fines and long prison sentences. Often black protesters were punched, pushed, and spit at by white mobs.

By the end of 1960, southern restaurants, theaters, hotels, and public facilities were dropping their "color barriers." Protesters that went to prison had their sentences thrown out by higher courts.

Freedom Riders

"I'm taking a ride on the Greyhound bus line.
I'm riding the front seat to Jackson this time.
Hallelujah, I'm traveling;
Hallelujah, ain't it fine?
Hallelujah, I'm traveling
Down Freedom's main line."

—Freedom Riders' Song

In 1961, interstate buses still discriminated against blacks. Bus stations had separate waiting rooms for blacks and whites. Blacks also had separate ticket windows, bathrooms, and lunch counters. To protest this, students in the South decided to go on "freedom rides." All were pledged to nonviolence.

The freedom riders met with violence all across the Deep South. Racist mobs burned buses and terrorized both black and white freedom riders. The police and National Guard units often looked the other way. Sometimes, ambulance drivers and hospitals would not treat wounded protesters. Many protesters were permanently disabled or killed during the freedom rides.

The problem continued to grow worse. President John F. Kennedy and his brother Robert, the Attorney General, decided to step in. The President ordered officials to cooperate with the freedom riders. But the governors of Alabama and Mississippi did not prevent their police from beating and arresting the riders. Many freedom riders were sent to maximum-security prisons. In response, Kennedy urged blacks to register to vote. As more blacks began to vote, some racist sheriffs and judges lost their jobs.

Eventually, the interstate buses gave equal treatment to all people. The freedom riders moved on to other projects.

Demonstrators trying to integrate public transportation in the South watch their bus burn after it was firebombed by a white mob.

The Birmingham Protests

The year 1963 was difficult for Martin Luther King, Jr., and the SCLC. George Wallace, a strict segregationist, had been elected governor of Alabama. Wallace stood in front of the doors to the University of Alabama and swore to keep blacks out of college forever. The FBI tapped King's phone and opened his mail. His campaign was losing popularity.

Alabama Governor George Wallace during his fight to preserve segregation in state public schools.

The year before, the city of Birmingham, Alabama, had closed parks, playgrounds, swimming pools, and golf courses. They closed these facilities so they would not have to allow blacks to use them. Stores that allowed blacks were hassled by Birmingham officials.

Dr. King decided to make Birmingham the next target of SCLC's protests. Before the protests, he toured the country making speeches and raising money for bail and defense. King also decided to allow children to protest. He thought the police would be less hostile toward them.

Children of Freedom

On May 2, 1963, thousands of black children marched in Birmingham. They ranged in age from six to 18. Around 900 people were arrested and taken to jail. The next day, more children marched. The city's police chief, Bill Connor, brought out police dogs and firemen. Connor ordered the firemen to turn their hoses on the children. Children were knocked down, thrown over cars, and slammed against curbs. Several others were attacked by dogs. That night, people around the country saw pictures of this brutality on the evening news.

Blacks in Birmingham were outraged. What began as a nonviolent protest soon erupted into riots. The Ku Klux Klan bombed King's hotel. Stores were burned. The number of casualties grew. President Kennedy feared that the rioting would spread across the country. He decided to take personal charge of the situation. Kennedy promised an end to segregation, and the rioting came to an end.

On June 19, 1963, Kennedy sent Congress the strongest civil rights bill in history. The bill empowered the attorney general to cut off funds to schools that would not allow blacks. It also outlawed southern laws that prohibited blacks from voting. Martin Luther King, Jr., wanted to make sure the bill passed. To demonstrate the power of black people, King decided to organize the biggest demonstration ever. They would take the cause of freedom to Washington, D.C.

TIMELINE

1947 Jackie Robinson becomes the first
African-American to play baseball in the
major leagues

1954 Supreme Court decides *Brown vs. Board of Education*;
orders schools to desegregate

1955 Rosa Parks refuses to give her seat on a city bus to a white man

1957 Gov. Faubus of Arkansas uses the Arkansas National Guard to
block black students from entering Central High in Little Rock

—— President Eisenhower orders the 101st Airborne Division to
force the integration of Central High

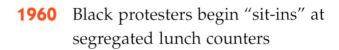

1960 Black protesters begin "sit-ins" at
segregated lunch counters

1961 Protesters begin "Freedom Rides" on interstate bus lines

1962 Arkansas fully integrates its schools

1963 Children march in Birmingham, AL

———— President Kennedy sends the strongest Civil Rights bill in history to Congress

———— Protesters march on Washington to demand equality for blacks; Martin Luther King, Jr. gives his famous "I Have a Dream" speech

———— President John F. Kennedy is assassinated

1964 Martin Luther King, Jr. wins the Nobel Peace Prize

1965 Malcolm X is assassinated

1968 Martin Luther King, Jr. is assassinated

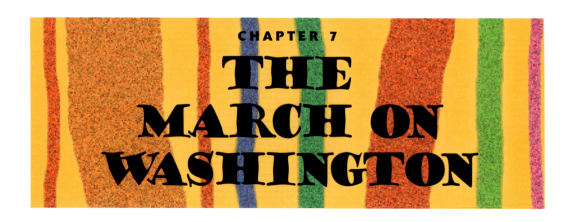

CHAPTER 7

THE MARCH ON WASHINGTON

Black groups chose August 28 as the date for the demonstration. Many leaders expected a few thousand people. Many members of Congress were opposed to the march, and to the demands of the black groups. President Kennedy tried to get black leaders to call off the march. He argued that if there were no trouble, the civil rights bill would have a better chance to pass. But when black leaders refused to call off the march, President Kennedy gave his support.

President Kennedy gives an address regarding the Alabama civil rights crisis.

Two thousand buses and 30 trains brought blacks to Washington from all over the country. The area between the Washington Monument and the Lincoln Memorial became a sea of people. Thousands of people waded in the Mall pond to cool off from the summer's heat. By the end of the day, 250,000 blacks and 60,000 whites had arrived to demand freedom and equal rights for black people. At the time, it was the largest demonstration in American history.

Musicians Bob Dylan and Mahalia Jackson sang to the crowd. Ministers, labor leaders, and black activists made speeches. John Lewis, one of the leading speakers, electrified the crowd. He said, "We shall splinter the segregated South into a thousand pieces, and put them back together in the image of God and democracy." Martin Luther King, Jr., gave his famous "I Have a Dream" speech. King's speech was full of hope and determination. He called for blacks and whites to live together in peace.

The March on Washington was a great success. There was no violence. On television, many Americans witnessed blacks and whites marching arm in arm for the first time. The march was a high point for millions of black people. It helped push the "freedom train" a little further down the track.

After the March

Just 18 days after the march, racial violence resumed. A bomb was thrown through a church window in Birmingham where black children were attending Bible class. Four children were killed. The country was reminded that the march was only one day in a long war against racism. Another blow came when John F. Kennedy was assassinated on November 22, 1963. Kennedy had been a strong supporter of black leaders. His death slowed the civil rights legislation in Congress.

Martin Luther King, Jr., giving his famous "I Have a Dream" speech.

In northern cities, many blacks were very angry about the brutal actions of white police officers. This anger led to a number of violent riots. Between 1964 and 1968, terrible riots broke out in many large American cities. These cities included New York, Los Angeles, Chicago, Cleveland, Baltimore, Newark, Detroit, and Washington. National Guard troops patrolled the streets in full battle gear. Buildings were burned and stores were looted. Snipers shot at police and firemen. Tempers on both sides flared out of control. Hundreds of people were wounded or killed.

CHAPTER 8

FREEDOM'S LEADERS

Malcolm X (1925–1965)

Civil Rights Activist

Malcolm X was born in Omaha, Nebraska. He was the seventh of eleven children. Malcolm's father, Reverend Earl Little, was a Baptist minister. He believed strongly in Marcus Garvey's movement for black independence. Reverend Little's ideas of black pride upset the local Ku Klux Klan. The Little family was driven out of town. They moved to Lansing, Michigan.

When Malcolm was four years old, a racist group in Lansing burned his family's house to the ground. Reverend Little rebuilt

Malcolm X shown here at a civil rights rally in 1963.

the home. When Malcolm was six, his father was murdered. Malcolm quit school in eighth grade and ran away. He went first to Boston, and then to Harlem. Soon he began committing crimes. At age 21, he was sent to prison for six years.

While in prison, Malcolm became interested in the Black Muslim movement. This movement began in Detroit in the 1930s. In the late 1950s, Black Muslims began to set up mosques and farms in several states. Soon other Muslim businesses, including bakeries and small factories, opened in black neighborhoods. Muslims ran the largest black newspaper in the country. They also ran schools, office buildings, banks, print shops, and apartment buildings. After he joined this movement, Malcolm dropped his last name. He began to call himself Malcolm X. Malcolm was released from prison in 1952. For the next 12 years, he taught the Muslim message and founded Muslim mosques. Soon he developed a large following.

The success of Malcolm X caused jealousy and friction within the Black Muslim movement. In December 1963, he was suspended from the Muslim church by its leader, Elijah Muhammad. Malcolm decided to begin his own group. He called it the Organization of Afro-American Unity (OAAU).

On February 15, 1965, Malcolm X's house was firebombed. On February 21, he was shot to death at a rally in New York City. Three Black Muslims were convicted of his murder. Thousands of black people mourned the death of Malcolm X. He was a leader in the revolution against racism and prejudice.

Martin Luther King, Jr. (1929–1968)

Civil Rights Activist

Martin Luther King, Jr., was born on January 15, 1929. His father was a minister at the Ebenezer Baptist Church in Atlanta, Georgia. His mother was a schoolteacher. At 15, King entered Morehouse

College in Atlanta. After graduation, he spent three years at a seminary. There he learned about Mohandas Gandhi's philosophy of nonviolence. King earned a Ph.D. from Boston University in 1955. Then he moved to Montgomery, Alabama, to become a minister. Soon after he arrived, he became a leader of the famous bus boycott.

In 1958, King wrote his first book, *Stride Toward Freedom.* In the early 1960s, he supported youth groups that organized sit-ins and freedom rides. In 1963, he was arrested in Birmingham, Alabama, for demanding an end to the Jim Crow laws.

When King was arrested in Birmingham, he was placed in solitary confinement. Meanwhile, local white ministers spoke out against the protests. King was disappointed in these ministers. In response, he decided to write his letter from the Birmingham jail. In this letter, King spoke of how racism caused hatred, disrespect, and poverty. He described the effect that racism had on children. King ended by asking for a peaceful end to segregation. Soon afterward, he was released from jail and the charges against him were dropped.

King went on to organize the March on Washington and push for the Civil Rights Act in Congress. In 1964, King received the Nobel Peace Prize. In 1965, he organized religious leaders from all faiths to

American civil rights leader Martin Luther King, Jr. receives the Nobel Peace Prize.

march in Selma, Alabama, where police had been brutally beating demonstrators. The violence in Selma caused President Lyndon Johnson to push for the Voting Rights Act of 1965. This act ensured that blacks could no longer be denied the right to vote.

In 1968, King went to Memphis, Tennessee, to help sanitation workers gain equal rights and better pay. On April 4, King walked onto the balcony of his hotel and was shot by James Earl Ray. When news of his death flashed across television screens, riots began in the black neighborhoods of most major American cities.

The death of Dr. Martin Luther King, Jr., is mourned by many to this day. He set an example for everyone who longs for equality, peace, and justice.

A Final Word

People like Rosa Parks and Martin Luther King, Jr., were great leaders in the struggle for civil rights. Many other brave people have also fought for equality, though their stories are less famous. If you want to learn more about these American heroes, visit your public library and look for books about black history. Even today, education is the key to freedom and equality.

T he most prominent events in the Civil Rights Movement took place in southern states like Alabama and Arkansas.

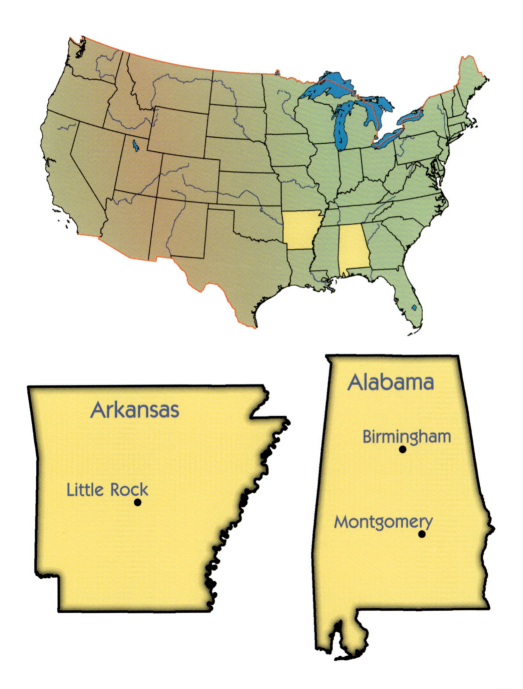

INTERNET SITES

African-American Odyssey—Library of Congress

http://lcweb2.loc.gov/ammem/aaohtml/

> *This Library of Congress site contains a history of blacks in America from slavery to civil rights. Check out pictures, links to other sites, and a collection of works by influential blacks in history.*

African-American History—Martin Luther King, Jr.

www.triadntr.net/~rdavis/king.htm

> *This site tells the story of Martin Luther King, Jr. and his leadership in the civil rights movement. Read a transcript of his famous speech, "I Have a Dream."*

Historic Places of the Civil Rights Movement

www.cr.nps.gov/nr/travel/civilrights/

> *See photographs and descriptions of famous places and events in the Civil Rights Movement. Follow the underground railroad, or check out the churches of Montgomery , Alabama.*

The FBI Freedom of Information Act Reading Room

http://foia.fbi.gov/

> *The official site to read the FBI's files. Read the FBI's files on the biggest investigations from the Mississippi Burning civil rights murders to the assassination of Dr. Martin Luther King, Jr.*

GLOSSARY

Boycott—To refuse to have anything to do with the products and services of a business or employer in order to force the acceptance of certain conditions. Blacks boycotted the city buses in Montgomery, Alabama so the bus company would allow blacks to sit wherever they chose.

Depression—A period of low economic activity marked by mass unemployment, deflation, and lack of investment. The Great Depression in America occurred after the stock market crash of 1929 and lasted through the mid-1930s.

Freedom Riders—Groups of black students in the south rode the interstate bus lines in an effort to desegregate the buses and terminals along the routes. These groups were met with great violence from whites, and often received no protection from the police. Many were injured and even killed riding for freedom.

Integrate—To allow black people into the same areas as white people. The first step towards integration in the south was the government forcing white schools to accept black students. Note: Desegregation is the same as integration.

Jim Crow Laws—A set of laws in the southern United States that called for blacks to have separate public facilities from whites. Public restrooms, restaurants, schools, and transportation were all designated for white or black use.

Ku Klux Klan—A secret organization founded in the southern United States after the civil war that advocated white rule by intimidating and violently attacking blacks.

The Little Rock Nine—The first black students to be integrated into the Arkansas school system at Central High in Little Rock. The students were subject to physical threats and violence from local white people who didn't want blacks in school with their children.

Lynching—The hanging or killing of someone by a mob as punishment for a presumed crime or offense.

Mosque—An Islamic house of worship.

NAACP—Short for the National Association for the Advancement of Colored People, the NAACP was an organization that sought equality for blacks, and often represented blacks in civil rights cases. The organization still exists today.

New Deal—President Roosevelt's plan to create new jobs for the poor and get the country out of the Great Depression through a series of new government programs like the Works Progress Administration and the Civilian Conservation Corps.

Segregate—To keep blacks separate from whites. Blacks were not allowed to attend white schools, sit in the white section of busses, or sit at lunch counters in restaurants where whites sat.

Soup Kitchen—A charitable place that gives soup, bread, and other essentials to the needy. Soup Kitchens were the prime source of meals for many poor and homeless people during the great depression.

INDEX